"Poems of gentle Dharma and observation touching on life's pain, joy and mystery from one who has looked long and deeply. A bedside reader for morning and night."

— **Ken Lenington**, MD, Order of Interbeing

"Bill Menza's poems on the Dharma are full of surprise and delight, yet they challenge and question the reader to contemplate deeply on what is most important in life."

— **Garrett Phelan**, True Shining Heart, artist, educator, editor and poet

"I first met Bill Menza at a retreat at Stonehill College in 2009. It was my first retreat, and I was filled with trepidation. Bill walked up to me and started talking with that Boston accent of his, all the while smiling and asking about me. My nervousness vanished and I knew I had met a kindred spirit, who was later to become my Dharma teacher. Bill's Zen poems are for the average person in everyday life, profound yet understandable, and convey his highly empathic understanding of everyone he meets."

— **Steve Swift**, Compassionate Insight of the Heart, Blue Cliff friend and neighbor

"I am forever grateful to William Menza for his kind teachings of the Five Mindfulness Trainings. His unmatchable poetry can also be found within the anthologies of *Poets for Peace* and *Immigration, Emigration and Diversity*. Menza is a fine poet who has helped join the East with the West."

— **Timothy F. Crowley**, poet

"Bill Menza lives life to the fullest, present and engaged with each moment. He looks deeply, sees to the heart of things and shares his insight via his wonderful smile, his engaged action and his poetry. Each of his poems is a beautiful jewel, exquisitely carved and come to light."

— **Theodate Lawlor**, True Land of Joy, practicing with the Still Water Sangha in Orono, Maine

"Bill's poems are a door to the Dharma. For the twenty years I have known him, he has leapt into every opportunity to deeply listen, to take copious notes, to reflect the Dharma teacher's right view distilled lessons. He illuminates all our lives with living practice. I am deeply grateful for his teachings... and his mischief."
— **Jindra Cekan**, PhD

"Brother Bill Menza, like his Dharma brother poet Thay Giac Thanh, offers his poems, humor and life as a gift for us all, effortlessly and lovingly sharing himself and his real life teachings with a glint in his eye and an infectious smile. Over the years, Bill has generously offered his poems to us in conversations, Dharma talks, emails and newsletters. For the first time, in this book, they now all have a true home, a true reflection of Bill's joy, insight, good humor and true heart. What a gift! Thanks, Dear Brother Bill!"
— **Jeanne Anselmo**, True Precious Hand, Holistic Nurse Educator & Dharma Sister

"Bill's poetry is right from his heart to the heart of the reader. His poems contain much wisdom, are easily understood, are simply lovely and illustrate what a wonderful teacher he is. I highly recommend this book!"
— **Ruth Fishel**, author of *The Joy of Aging Mindfully* and other titles

DHARMA RAIN
BRINGS FLOWERS

selected poems by
William P. Menza

The Whole Salamander & Friends LLC
Publishing Cooperative

Dharma Rain Brings Flowers
by William P. Menza
Copyright 2015

Published with The Whole Salamander & Friends LLC
www.thewholesalamander.com
Athena Books of Fairview, North Carolina, USA
ISBN 978-0983534679
Cover image supplied by Fotolia

Do all of this for those who are not able to.

Foreward

Bill Menza was my dear friend, counselor, and role model. As a loving brother on the path, over the course of many years he touched me deeply through his persistent teachings about, and honest behavioral demonstrations of love based on the Dharma.

Bill's unwavering reliance on the Dharma to encourage others to wake up and to love and serve others shone like a bright beam of light. My growth and clear seeing was enhanced by his frequent reminder that taking refuge in the Three Jewels — the Buddha, the Dharma, and the Sangha — is all that one needs for healing and transformation in this life.

When encountering Bill, one was assured that through his teaching, his friendship, and other vehicles, one would receive life-affirming gifts. He understood and taught that. the connection, understanding, and acceptance that we all so long for *always* flow to us and through us when we share our love, compassion, and generosity with all sentient beings.

For years, Bill and approximately 15 other sangha brothers and sisters met Sunday mornings at a brother's farm near Tampa, Florida, to study the Dharma, enjoy the beautiful scenery, and pick oranges generously made available by the farm's owners. During these gatherings, one could count on Bill's deep, penetrating contributions during the discussion period. We all marveled at his copious note-taking, assured that he would use them to share insights and wisdom for years. Bill turned picking oranges into yet another loving exercise as he always picked an extra bag or two to take back to Sarasota to share with others.

No matter the topic: the death of a loved one; racism; an inhumane prison system; the Holocaust; the Charleston, SC massacre; Engaged Buddhism and the prerequisites for activism based on Right View; the wounded child; his own "demons" or anything I or anyone within the group became stuck on, Bill always found time to connect, to care, and to teach. Moreover, no matter the location, the Tampa Practice Center, Blue Cliff Monastery, Plum Village, cyberspace, or elsewhere, Bill made himself available for teaching and sharing the Dharma. While conversations with Bill were always welcomed and beneficial, for years Bill quietly and persistently created and nourished yet another vehicle, his wonderful Dharma poems.

On September 10, 2010, I received four poems from Bill which reminded me of my good fortune of having received many others from him over the years. It was probably then that I first thought about how a book of his poetry could also benefit many others. In early 2015, exactly two weeks after his cancer diagnosis, an email exchange between us resulted in the launching of a long-overdue book project.

Deeply grateful for the years-long Dharma poetry teachings that he'd so generously shared with me, on March 17, 2015, I asked if he'd ever considered publishing some of his poems. He responded with the subject line: "Hi Sandy; am I dreaming!!!! hugs and poems" and went on to write, "Your words are some very strong good medicine. I am feeling real good now. A book of poems so they can tell others about the Dharma has been my life-time dream. Let's look into this. Over the next few weeks I might not be able to help a lot with such a project. Maybe especially when chemo treatment starts. But would do what I can. Yes, please share my poems as you see fit and useful to spread the Dharma. I will send you more poems to put to good Dharma use."

Shortly thereafter, Bill sent 176 poems. I contacted Beth DeLap, of The Whole Salamander Publishing Cooperative, and Ken Lenington, Beth's husband and Bill's dear sangha brother. Ken read and edited every poem, Beth agreed to involve her masterful editing and publishing skills, and the project took off.

During the days that he was critically ill and his body deteriorated, Bill continued to send detailed, intimate, loving emails that shared information about his various ailments so that others might learn and possibly take steps to alleviate their own present or anticipated suffering. Always giving. He labeled his many doctors, other help providers, and his beloved wife Alicia as true Bodhisattvas. Always grateful. As a participant on the phone sangha, Bill continued to teach and share until he was too weak to continue. Always loving.

Ultimately, 210 poems were included in a proof copy of *Dharma Rain Brings Flowers* that brother Bill was able to enjoy for two weeks before he left. Writing that the book was his baby, Bill was pleased that the words that he had so diligently and lovingly worked with for many years might, in fact, benefit others and help to foster understanding and compassion among sentient beings, and love of the Dharma.

Thank you dear friend Bill for being all that you were, and for having given all that you gave to your fellow brothers and sisters throughout the world. You are the true embodiment of the concept and practice of Interbeing, and of the fact that we Inter-are. May the Dharma Rain in your book water the seeds of wisdom and compassion for countless people from all walks of life and on all loving paths throughout the world.

With love, joy, and ease,
Sandy Garcia, PhD, JD
Source of True Clarity

Prologue

In early 2003, William "Bill" Menza was invited to teach the Dharma by Dhyana Master Trung Quang Nhat Hanh (Thich Nhat Hanh) of the 43rd generation of the Lam Te School and the 9th generation of the Lieu Quan Dharma Line. The invitation, ritualized as the Lamp Transmission ceremony, included the following two poems:

BY BILL TO THICH NHAT HANH
Boats of compassion have made us seaworthy,
So we are not tossed about and drowned
In the high seas of reactivity,
But sail calm waters to places with laughing children.

BY THICH NHAT HANH TO BILL
True Understanding brings us to the other shore.
From the depths of the earth echoes
    the sound of the rising tide.
Refreshing is the plum flower of
    the everlasting green spring.
Each footstep reveals a daffodil blossom.

January 12, 2003 at Plum Village, France

DHARMA RAIN
BRINGS FLOWERS

WHY NOT LIVE UNCERTAIN

Why not live uncertain,
As impermanence is everywhere,
Nothing is excluded,
For all things arise and pass away.
This is the Shining Path.
Those who understand this
Are free of suffering.

THE FIRST THING IN THE MORNING

When you wake up in the morning
Enter calm abiding right away,
For all is a dream,
Played out by causes and conditions.
Feel the sun,
Smell the flowers,
Breathe in and breathe out.
Aspire to help everyone to be free like this,
To aspire to help everyone to be free like this.

DHARMA, NOT DRAMAS

Don't get involved in the dramas
In your mind, your ego's
Or other people's,
In the news, TV, radio, movies,
On the cell or regular phone calls,
Smartphone, iPad, postal letters,
Email, Twitter or Facebook,
Those in front of you or far away.
Those high drama soapbox fantasies
Filled with conflict, egotism,
Cruelty, inhumanness.
This is not the Dharma.

SIT LIKE THIS

Meditation transforms consciousness,
Thus make your mind itself an object of
concentration,
Be aware of how your mind functions.
Then empty it,
So there is pure conscious awareness.
Sit like this.

FACE YOUR FEAR SQUARELY

Why not face your fear directly
So you can know this phantom,
This mind delusion,
That simply arises and passes away.
But yet, let it go,
So it unfolds into the Great Unfolding,
The Great Impermanence.

OUR DREAMS, OUR CHILDREN
St Anne's Lake, Reston, VA, Aug. 12, 2006

We try to have our children live our dreams,
But they find their own,
And how best to live them.
So pass the time
Leaving it to the flow.

WANTING AND NOT WANTING A FEELING

Wanting a certain feeling,
Like being happy, accepted, or liked,
And not unhappy, excluded, incompetent,
Does not make sense.
As feelings come and go,
Like clouds in a windy sky,
Like apparitions appearing, disappearing.
Best to focus on your breathing.

THE QUEST

The quest is not to do away with your "I,"
But to exchange "I" with "other,"
Since there is no self,
But only this delusion.
To know this is to be one
With everything.

BODHICITTA

The curtain of delusion slightly lifts,
The grip of the ego lessens,
The apparition of self recedes.
It starts with wanting to be free,
Or for another to be liberated from suffering,
Like a flash of lightning, this mind of kind
understanding.
These are your greatest moments,
Honor and live them fully.

TAKING CARE OF DEMONS

When your demons of greed, anger, pride, regrets
And other wounds rise up in your mind,
Take good care of them,
As you would your son or daughter,
For that is what they want,
To rest in your calm abiding,
With its marvelous illumination, wise compassion.
I vow to take good care of my demons
So they don't disturb my mind's natural cheerful
disposition.

WORDS ARE A MAGIC TRICK

When people tell you something,
Usually you believe what they say,
Because you normally believe what you hear.
It's automatic.
But what are words?
You cannot touch these apparitions,
The magic show.
So why react strongly or at all?
With fear, anger, regret, jealousy, envy?
To words.
Just let them be.
While you rest in your direct experience,
Beyond them.

IT CONTINUES

The battle continues
Day in and day out
Each moment,
With ego-self,
And since there is no death,
It will go on forever.
Then best to be good friends,
So we can help each other
Rest free in calm abiding.

OUR ZEN TEACHER

He brings Dharma
Wrapped in mindful smiles
So flowers bloom

THEY ARE CALLING YOU

The Ancestors are calling you,
That is why you are here,
Where you find yourself.
They need your presence,
For those present.

THE BEAUTIFUL YOU

Just like a Buddha,
You're a good person,
Kind, understanding, and gentle,
Thinking beautifully,
Speaking and acting with beauty,
Showing the beautiful in you.

THREE BREATH-BOWS
(FOR EMERGENCY STOPPING)

Stop where you are,
Whatever you are doing,
Join your palms,
Close your eyes,
Breathe in and out
   three times,
While bowing deeply,
To your ancestors,
Loved ones,
Teachers,
Enemies,
Those suffering.
The Buddha inside.

(Repeat throughout the day.)

YOU ARE ONLY A BREATH AWAY

You are only a breath away,
Just like in sitting meditation
From fear, worry, anger, regret,
Peace or joy,
Heaven or hell,
Moment to moment,
Breath to breath.
So simple,
Just breathe away.

ANCHORS AWEIGH!

Watch the changing view,
A magic show
24/7
Day and night
Now this
Now that,
Depending on this cause,
That condition.
Sad fearfulness,
Happy joyfulness,
Anxious confusion,
Solid stability.
Oh! how they change!
Moment to moment!
Have I gone mad!
Mindful breathing
    is my anchor.
Only this mindful step is real.
Anchors aweigh!

HAVE YOU EVER GOTTEN A THOUGHT

That would not leave you alone?
No matter what you did,
It kept coming back,
Like a bad dream,
A haunting ghost,
Demanding your attention,
Taking possession of your mind.
Maybe all she wants is to be held
Tenderly, as a mother does
Her sick or troubled child;
And lullabied to sleep.
Breathe in his fear, confusion,
Hurt and pain,
Breathe out kind understanding,
To set him free.

DO NOT ENGAGE

With whatever comes before you
Unless you are abiding
   in your original mind.
This means any thoughts or feelings,
Perceptions, bodily sensations,
And consciousness.
Just let them be,
As you calmly abide
Reflecting things as they are.

TRUE MIND

Entering this meditation hall
I see my true mind,
And vow that once I sit down
All disturbances will stop.

Before entering this sacred place,
I remove my shoes
To walk sacredly,
To leave my sorrows at the door,
Like so many others before me.

As I watch my thoughts come and go
Like clouds in windy sky
Or caught in heavy rains,
Conscious breathing is my anchor.

As I breathe in---
I know I am breathing in this breath.
Breathing out I know
All the rest is just "thinking."

60,000 THOUGHTS A DAY
(PSYCHOLOGISTS TELL US)

What does your mind-body do most of the time?
Do you really know what you are doing?
Don't think!
Don't think!
Tell me!
Tell me!
Speak from your gut!
Not your head!
Speak with an empty mind!
Speak with your whole being!

HOW NOT TO THINK

First, most of your thinking is useless.
60,000 thoughts a day,
And most of them repeats.
Take a full mindful step completely,
Then another and another,
With no end.
So you are walking without thinking.

WHAT WAS YOUR MIND LIKE BEFORE STEPPING ON THE PATH?

What was your mind like
Before stepping on the Path?
Small town working class Catholic boy's,
Filled with beliefs, feelings, delusions,
Thoughts feeding on thoughts,
From parents, teachers, ancestors,
And numerous others.

And now?
They are still with me,
And not with me.
For I have the eyes, ears, and mind
Of the Buddha, Dharma, and Sangha.
They appear and disappear,
It is the same with all phenomena.

Only each footstep on the Path is real,
Bringing me back to awareness,
Of my unborn Buddha Mind
In the present moment.

DO NOT BE MINDLESS

You must bring your mind home,
So it will not go astray and get lost.
Once home you can lose your mind,
So you can be light and free
In present moment wonders.

If you think,
Your mind will be caught and imprisoned
By your thoughts.

Place your mind at your hara,
Three fingers width below your naval,
So it does not wander.
Here the mind removes thoughts
Becoming no-mind,
Resting in the awareness
That does not think.

Do this every free moment
To condition the mind
To come to this condition by itself.
Do not be mindless.

PILGRIMS

We are pilgrims,
On a pilgrimage,
Learning anew,
About ancient people and places.
A great adventure
Into new experiences.
This is the way
From birth to death.
This is the Way.
Om Mani Padme Hum.

MIND COCKROACHES

The mind is the source of all confusion.
We think too much,
Obsess and try to control,
Have addictions,
The mind cockroaches.
Wake up!
Turn the light on!
Practice your mindful breathing!

DOES THE MIND HIDE THE TRUTH?

It is difficult to know,
For the mind is the source of all confusion.
A most wonderful kaleidoscope
Of thinking, consciousness, perception,
Feelings and sensations.
Add continuous conditioning by family,
Community, education, and what have you.
What is one to do?
Continue,
One mindful step at a time,
As you look deeply,
With compassion.

ORIGINAL NIRVANA MIND

Resting in my original mind,
My original mind only,
My unborn Buddha mind,
Enlightenment reigns.

CALM ABIDING

Your job, my job is to be light and free.
To find calm abiding inside ourself,
By letting go of everything,
With no exceptions.
Just like when we are sitting on the meditation
cushion.
Letting go of accomplishing,
Obtaining, getting, doing,
By breathing into abiding calmly,
So there is only being,
Then we let go of that too.

EGOHOLIC

First saying: "I'm an egoholic."
Might be the first step of many
On the Path to an enlightened mind.
For "me," "mine,"
"I need," "I want," "I must be (whatever),"
Are heavy intoxicants,
Which cloud and make the mind more confused.
So to safeguard against this,
When in a group or with another,
Even yourself,
Begin with: "I'm an egoholic."

TELL MANAS TO PRACTICE MINDFULNESS

Tell your ego to practice mindful breathing,
Especially when he appears in full splendor.
Tell him to practice mindful walking
To be calm and stable.
Tell him you understand,
And will take care of everything,
And that everything is fine as it is,
For it is as it is,
With non-self interbeing.

STOPPING IS THE PRACTICE

Stop your fear, worries, regrets,
Old age and death too,
With restful mindfulness,
So your perceptions and feelings
Bring compassionate understanding,
With joyful well-being
At the depths of our consciousness----
This is transformation at the base.

MINDFUL BREATHING IS THE PRACTICE

It goes like this,
Just sit and feel your breath 100 percent
    as it goes in and out,
Until you are your breathing,
With no future or past,
No thoughts,
No to do,
Only being.

THE GAZE IS OUTWARD

The gaze is outward
Away from the self,
Toward the other.
If judgment enters,
Egocentricity is engaged,
The view gets small,
The mind gets small,
The heart gets small.
To leave these prison walls,
Ask: "How can I help you?"

RIVER OF EMOTIONS

The river of emotions flows 24/7
    day and night,
    without end,
As I sit on the bank watching
Them flow by,
One after the other,
This feeling,
Now that one.
Feelings are not a problem,
As they constantly change.
What a magic show!

UPSET EMOTIONS ARE LIKE SMALL CHILDREN

Upset emotions,
Are small children
Needing your motherly love,
Fatherly attention,
To be held tenderly,
While being lullabied to sleep.

IT'S JUST A FEELING

Don't turn away,
Push down,
Deny or hide it.
Face and look directly,
To feel this feeling.
Embrace and hold it close.
To see-feel its texture,
Visceral sensations,
In your body.
Go there and tell her,
"I know you are not me."
"But just like a passing dream."
"Everything will be just fine."

WHEN LONELY

When lonely go inside yourself,
Knowing so many love you,
Including me,
We all want you to be well and happy.
"Breathing-in I go inside myself,
Where there are beautiful trees,
Clear streams, singing birds, and sun shine.
Breathing-out I feel safe.
I enjoy going to my refuge."*

*from a Plum Village song

YOUR HURT FEELINGS

Do your feelings get hurt easily?
Do they bruise readily?
Getting black and blue inside?
Because you want people to like you?
Treat you in a special way?

What's the answer?
Don't blame,
Take a mindful walk,
While looking deeply,
To see the rising and passing away
    of everything each moment,
And be with kindred spirits.

THEN WHERE ARE THEY

Sit quietly.
Just be.
Just continue.
"It" will become clear.
There will be understanding.
Thoughts come and go.
Emotions arise and pass away.
"Show me them," asked Master Bankei.
"I can't," you say.
"Then where are they?"

HOW TO WASH AWAY WORRIES AND FEARS, ANXIETIES, SORROWS, AND REGRETS

Go where nature is more present than not.
Where you can be aware of trees, clouds,
Grass, flowers, birds,
Rivers, lakes, or the sea.
Smell, hear, touch them,
Visualize their aliveness,
Until you are one
Feeling their strength,
With the freshness of the earth flowing
Through every cell in your body-mind,
Cleaning away your worries, fears,
Anxieties, sorrows and regrets.

TO BE A FREE PERSON

We are all prisoners,
Caught by our thoughts and feelings,
Beliefs, views,
Opinions,
Reactions,
Compulsions,
Addictions,
Conditioning,
Ignorance,
Delusions.
But we can think, speak and act like a free person,
On the Path to liberation.

FREE PRISONER

Continue your mind work,
The feelings work,
Each day each moment.
To know and understand.
Some are light and free,
Others heavy and dark.
But at least you are aware,
So you are a free prisoner.

THE QUESTION IS?

How directly close,
How intimate can you be
With what you find each morning when you wake up,
Or before you go to sleep at night,
Or unexpectedly sometime during the day?

You know that feeling of unsatisfactoriness,
Discontent,
Irritation,
Discomfort,
Regret,
Failure,
Not measuring up,
The blues or depression,
Lonely loneliness,
Boredom,
A sense of unhappiness.

You know, with people not as you want them,
Or places or circumstances,
Or you yourself.

You know: old age, sickness, and death.
World famine,
Corruption, cruelty, brutality,
Torture, rape, war,
Hatred, greed.

You know, with the raging fires of birth and death.
With the sense of an endless void within?

Before you reach for companionship,
The TV or radio "on" button,
The telephone,
Or looking at your computer screen,
Or going shopping,
Or to a movie,
Or eating something.

Without evaluating or judging.
Without reacting in any way.

Stand naked
With the nakedness
Of whatever comes up,
Or appears in or around you.

Here is the answer:
Repeat after me:

"The mind can go in a hundred directions.
But on this beautiful path I walk in peace.
Breathing in, I know I am breathing in.
Breathing out, I know I am breathing out." *

                        * *Thich Nhat Hanh*

GENEROSITY

Generosity is the opposite of greed,
One of the three poisons.
The antidote is compassion,
Seeing the other as you,
With no pity, no victim,
    for this exalts you,
    brings separation,
    and more suffering.
So embrace yourselves
With understanding love
Until even oneness disappears.

LITTLE FLOWERS

They discard them so easily---
My little flowers,
Given with so much sincerity.

A little hello,
A kind word,
A comment of interest,
A small smile.

They just let them fall to the roadside,
To be trampled on by business,
And self-absorption.

If such thoughtlessness affects your gardening,
"Look inside yourself." some would say.
"You are too attached to your flowers."

So should I stop giving flowers?
Loving-kindness says no.
Also, those who nurture and harvest flowers
Are one with the sun, rain, and earth,
And this might be the only flower
Given to her in a very long time.

A flower to you my dear ones,
Especially you who trample them.

SHOULDN'T

When someone says,
"You shouldn't have said or did that."
Defense is automatic and immediate.
"I did nothing wrong. I was right."
"You are not correct."
This is the usual way,
To disown and push away.
Instead embrace the feeling,
To know and understand her,
And to take good care of him.
Breathing in, I am aware of this feeling.
(Of not liking to be told I was wrong,
When I was not).
Breathing out, I relax this feeling.
Breathing in, I am aware of this relaxed feeling.
Breathing out, I let this feeling go,
Breathing in, I am light and free.
Breathing out, I am light and free.

NO ROAD RAGE

In front cars,
In back,
To the right and left,
Just passing thoughts and emotions,
As in sitting meditation.
Bubbles arising and passing away.
There is no judgment or attachment,
Like still water,
Reflect things as they are,
Like a solid mountain
Sitting in my car.

RUTHLESSNESS

I have tried to be ruthless,
As it is highly valued,
The ruthless rise to the top.
Culturalism,
Capitalism,
Socialism,
Darwinism,
Patriotism,
Individualism,
Egoism.
But I failed badly,
So I continue on the Path.

WHAT IS A LAMP TRANSMISSION?

The Lamp is all about your teacher,
    and ancestors,
    the Buddha.
Not you,
Not me,
An embryo,
They help to grow,
At its own pace and time,
Helping others
Along the Way.

So you are here
To explain the Dharma.
No, reflect it
As a living mirror,
Showing your Buddha nature,
So others can see theirs.
Please take a good look
By holding the lamp close.

EGOISM REIGNS

Egoism rules,
Controls,
Directs,
Captures
Each thought
And effort.

What about me?
What's in it for me?
Take care of me first.
You deserve to be first.
You worked for it.

It's a ruthless world.
Eat or get eaten.
You have to step on others
    to get ahead.

Such delusion is the ego way,
Whereas the Way to freedom shows
Interbeing oneness everywhere.

WHO'S IN CONTROL?

You sure aren't,
You can't even control what thoughts your mind
has,
    or does not.
Don't forget old age, sickness, and death.
So many causes and conditions.
Add constant changing impermanence.
It means you'll never get it all together.
But each step can be solid and stable
    as your foot touches the ground.

I'M PRACTICING BEING PRESENT

I'm practicing being present,
Present here and now,
For my breathing in and out,
All my body sensations,
My mind thinking,
My feelings and perceptions,
For all my difficulties,
And those of others.
I'm practicing being present
To the constant changing impermanence,
I'm practicing emptiness.

CONNECTING CONNECTIONS

It is all about connecting connections,
Which are called relationships,
Which need to be cultivated, nourished,
Taken good care of,
With your loved ones and others,
The Buddha, Dharma, and Sangha,
Or they might dry up and wither.
So start your gardening work right now,
Don't delay.

THE FIVE MINDFULNESS TRAININGS ARE LIKE A CLOAK

The Five Mindfulness Trainings are like a cloak
  to wrap around yourself
So that you can be mindful
  of what you are doing.
So that you can be awake
  in the present moment
  with all its wonders.
So that you can be in the Pure Land
  with all its happinesses.
So you can let go of everything
  and be light and free,
Being the Buddha that you are.

TRAUMA EQUALS MORE TRAUMA

Be careful with your helping others
With their suffering and pain,
With their traumas,
For when you learn about it,
Feel, see, and understand,
You are part of it,
And so a second trauma has happened.
And when you share it with another,
Another trauma and so on.....

Be aware,
Take mindful remedies,
Like when breathing in, I am aware of this trauma,
Breathing out, I feel healing love for myself and
her,
Breathing in, I let this trauma go,
Breathing out, I feel light and free.

GIVING DHARMA TALKS

Be ego free,
As much as you can,
Although it's so hard and difficult,
Not to own the talk about to be given,
The discussion about to be facilitated,
Even though you know they are not you,
And that you are here for your ancestors,
Spiritual and blood teachers,
For the Buddha,
To share the Dharma,
Even if no one shows up,
Or just one person.
For the Bodhisattva Way is always,
Trying to help transform and free
    all beings,
Present and not present
    at this moment.

IT'S ALL ABOUT LIFTING UP

Lifting up and out,
Not wallowing in,
Not being caught
By suffering,
No matter what kind,
For it's found everywhere,
Nothing is without it.
Birth, getting old and sick,
Death, grief, despair,
Association with the unpleasant,
Separation from the pleasant,
Impermanence.

So follow the Way
To liberation and freedom.

WE ALL NEED SUPPORT

It starts when you were born,
Your mother, father, grandparents,
Aunts, uncles, cousins,
Neighbors, teachers, and so many others
Supported you and do so now,
For there is the interbeing of things.

You exist,
And are able to do what you do,
Because of others.

So it is important for you
To reach out and help others,
Just as they did (or did not),
Especially to those who need it most.
Start with yourself,
Find a way each day.
They need you.

LOOK CAREFULLY

And maybe you'll notice
How often quickly, easily
You are disturbed or upset,
Irritated, maybe angry
Because things are not the way
You think they should be.
Political leaders, neighbors,
Family members, loved ones
Say or do something
Not how you think they should.
The weather is not to your liking.
Your car breaks down, and so on.
It is like a poison
Eating away at your peace
    and tranquility.
The antidote is to know
People, places or things
Are the way they are
Because they are.
And focus on their wonders.

NOT WANTING BRINGS UNHAPPINESS

It occurred to me
On a most beautiful day,
Which was holding me so tenderly,
While viewing a radiant blue heaven
With puffy white clouds,
Warmed by a rising sun,
With singing birds in the background,
And colored autumn trees in front,
That perhaps the main cause of my unhappiness is,
My not wanting things to be the way I find them,
That is, my not accepting
People, places, and things as they are.
While knowing too
There is impermanence everywhere
Transforming it all,
Including my not-wanting discontent.
So Happy Days are here and now!
Everything is changing!

SITTING AND WALKING MEDITATION FOR OTHERS

Everyday sitting and walking meditations are not for me,
I do them for those who cannot,
Because of their pain and anguish,
Their fear and regrets,
For those hungry and with no place to sleep,
Who are beaten, raped, and tortured,
Denied medical care or an education,
For those filled with hatred, greed, and delusion.
I sit and walk for transformation
I sit and walk for revolution
For you and me.

DAYS OF MINDFULNESS

Can be lazy days,
I learned at Plum Village.
I was very startled at first,
Fearful about what not to do,
With an empty day
With a no agenda day.
So I asked if someone would like
To go walking on country roads.
We passed fields of sunflowers,
Farmers harvesting fruits and vegetables,
To a café in a small French town,
To have a cup of coffee.
Then walked back
With a little conversation,
As we enjoyed the warm sun,
The clouds in the sky.
Others wrote poems or letters,
Painted pictures,
Enjoyed a silent meal.

How sweet those lazy days.
How wonderful to just hang-out
With nature, family, friends,
Yourself.

A LAZY DAY

I have a lazy time here and there,
When my mind thinks no thoughts,
My emotions feel light and free,
And my consciousness is aimlessness.
It can be an unfamiliar place.

AWAKENESS

It's all about being awake,
Not lost in thoughts,
Or caught by delusions.
It's about awareness.
Call it mindfulness,
With focused concentration.
Use whatever words help
To know your mind-body,
In the moment,
Like an inquisitive child
With beginner's mind,
Having more adventures.

ENTER THE BARDO

At times life's turbulence fragments us
And we enter the bardo.
A time charged with great potential for
transformation.
Liberation, enlightenment, nirvana are near.
We stand at the edge of the precipice.
Disconnected from ourselves,
Lost in uncertainty,
Anxious, restless, paranoid.
Panic visits often.
Suspense and ambiguity rule.
The mind shifts in and out
Of confusion and clarity,
Bewilderment and insight,
Sanity and insanity.
All are flowering opportunities
For changing consciousness
To a stable awareness
Of the nature of the mind
With its changing thoughts and emotions
And empty interbeing.

WHAT IS AGING?

Relentless changing impermanence,
Ending in a return to where you came from.
You might say: "Getting closer to the earth."
I am of the nature to get old, sick, and die.
"Hello Mother Earth,
I'm coming home."

STRUGGLE DAILY

Yes, the struggle is daily,
To change your nature.
Ego nature,
Family nature,
Cultural nature,
Human nature.
No easy task.
So sometimes,
I just breathe in and out!

AFTER A SUICIDE

Written after learning about the suicide death of a foreign student from China who had studied in the USA.

This is incredible, sad news!
I am here for you.
For your families
For all the young and old women and men
With great stress and despair.
I breathe in all your pain and suffering,
And breathe out lightness, freshness,
Kindness, and healing.
The trees, rivers, green plants,
Mother Earth do the same.
We will continue breathing like this,
Until we cannot do so anymore.
May you be healed,
Healthy and happy,
Feeling our love and understanding.
Sincerely yours,
Your ancestors.

KILLING PRISONERS

First the plan to kill,
Then the Order to kill,
Then the killing.
One, two, three; it's so easy.

I only urged 12 people
To tell the judge, to kill him,
After he suffers on death row.
There can never be enough suffering.

Said the psychopath.
One dressed as a judge.
Another as a prosecutor.
And the jurors with their delusions.

This is the political way.
More violent cruel brutality.
More inhuman inhumaneness.
The dark side grows.

The brute is king.
Mindlessness reigns.
Savagery triumphs.
Civilization is lessened.
This is the death penalty.

How wonderful these mechanical killings.
Hail "Brave New World." We are there.

Hail "1984." We are here.
Stick him with a needle; or electrocute.

Suicide is a mind-state; murder is too.
Closed minds that don't know what to do.
But to kill, but to kill.
Where do these minds come from?

Hate is a concept with many attachments.
Hate closes off; chokes out life.
Hate leaves no room to see good in the other.
Where does hate mind come from?

Hate is revenge. Revenge is punishment.
Punishment is violence. Violence is killing.
Killing is the death penalty.
Where does this killing mind come from.

Tell them, "I know you are suffering."
Tell them, "I am here for you."
Be truly present for them, in the present moment.
Like still water, reflect things as they are.

Listen mindfully to release their pain.
Help them to become awake,
To the causes of their suffering.
And you to yours.

NO-DEATH

We are
With you
At this time
Of no birth
And no death.
For there is
Only transformation.
Returning
To what we were once.
To the source
Of what we are.
For now here
There is only
The Path or Way,
To oneness.

TONGLEN

I see pain
In others or in me,
There is no escape,
We are caught.
What then?
Push it away
And its power grows.
So I breathe it in,
Letting it ride on my breath.
A heavy dark cloud,
Burning with fire and smoke.
Then I breathe it out
From my lungs, nose, mouth,
Every pore in my body,
As white healing sunlight,
Soft white clouds.
I do this with my whole body-mind,
There is no thinking,
Only healing compassion.

THE ESTES PARK RETREAT

Awareness surrounded me,
There was absolute stillness,
As Thay taught:
"You cannot be a practitioner and not do the
practice."
With this everyone sat up more straight.
We wanted to do our best.
Although we had not asked for the opportunity,
We stepped up and embraced the gift,
Rooted in our practice,
Just as Thay's absence was his Dharma talk,
This was our Dharma talk,
Along with that of the monastics'
With their stability, devotion, and love,
The Dharma marvelously illuminating us.

WHAT IS BEGINNING ANEW?

It is a constant practice,
Just like sitting and walking meditations,
Each day, each hour, each moment
Of just stopping
And coming back.

Back to what?
Back to pure awareness
Of what is here and now.
Without any add-ons
Of thinking thoughts,
Of feeling emotions,
Of wanting and not wanting,
Of having and not having.

What is the name of this place?
Call it what you want.
The place of pure awareness.
The place of no-thoughts.
The place of mindful understanding.
The place of marvelous illumination.
My true home.
Or maybe: my unborn Buddha mind.

Stop and rest here often,
Keep coming back,
Until you never leave.

WE THINK WE SHOULD BE HAPPY

We think we should be happy,
And when this is not happening we get upset,
Try to get away from our unsatisfactoriness.
We close off, shut down,
Try to fix things.
When it would be better to just let go,
And be,
With the dissatisfaction,
The uncomfortableness,
The uncertainty,
The confusion.
For this connects you to others
And reality.
There is nothing wrong with being unhappy.

EIGHT WORLDLY DHARMAS ARE NOT ME

My purpose is not to receive praise,
Nor to be famous and liked,
Nor to only seek my happiness.
It is not to gain anything,

But to be the medicine,
That transforms anger into love,
Greed into generosity,
Ignorance into understanding.

So we cross the ocean of suffering
        to the other shore,
Where there is the laughing of children.

MORNING WALKING MEDITATION

My morning walking meditation
Begins with opening my door and stepping outside
To say "Good Morning" to the sky and clouds,
The pine trees and birds,
The morning sun or falling rain,
And the nearby and distant hills and mountains,
Which I look at as I walk down Ledgewood Drive,
Passing houses still asleep.
At the bottom a small pond, frogs croak: "Hello."
Then it's left along the railroad tracks,
On which I balance
Seeing how far I can walk without falling off,
Just as I did as a small boy.
The tracks pass a gas station, bookstore,
A small park with a statue of long-ago abolitionist
Harriet Wilson,
Who died near Boston.
Then I pass by a large pond with many water lilies,
And go down the street with the police station,
Which circles back to the high steepled First
Congregational Church on Union St.
Then I walk toward the oval at the town's center,
Passing the Yankee diner with breakfast patrons,

And come to a bridge where I stop
To watch the water flow over a small dam.
Then down a small alley close to the dam,
Where I stop to watch the flowing water
   some more.
The walk continues through the bank's parking lot,
Where I have another view of the pond and lilies.
Then it's up High Street going by old houses,
Granite stone walls, oak trees,
And back to the railroad tracks,
Then left onto Route 13 for a few steps,
Passing behind the auto body shop,
And the birthing center,
Then up steep Webster St.
And then the long climb up Prospect St.
With its manicured houses and lilac bushes,
Including the 1800's Civil War Hutchinson Family
   singers' house,
And pass the newly built small house on the left.
Enroute there are birds and flowers to say
   "Hello" to,
Or to neighbors taking a walk or going to work.
Now and then I read a passage from a
   meditative book,
Then reflect and meditate on what was said,

At times stopping when the church bell rings,
To recite the mantra:
"Breathing in, I know with each step
    I am one with all I meet."
"Breathing out, I know with each step I am home."

GO BACK INSIDE

Go back, go back,
And capture that mind-body feeling,
In that place
Of being light and free,
When you are mesmerized
By the warm sun,
The falling rain or snow,
Eating a good meal,
Having a good cup of coffee,
Or looking at the blue sky,
Or bright stars,
Or being with a loved one,
A mindful breath or step.
Recall that place inside,
And rest there,
Especially when difficulties arise.

ASK YOURSELF RIGHT NOW

Ask yourself right now
Of what value, use, or purpose
Is your thinking,
The thoughts you are having
Right now?
You'll discover, not much.
So a better use of your mind
Would be to see and enjoy
The wonders and miracles around you,
And that you and others are,
And to fill your mind
With similar good thoughts.

If this is difficult,
Just fill your mind with these words:
"Breathing in, I know I am breathing in."
"Breathing out, I know I am breathing out."

REPLACE THEM ALL

Yes, replace all those useless thoughts
With mindful awareness
Or something much better,
And more pleasant.
A mindful breath or step,
Mindful relaxing and smiling.
Or being empty nothingness.
Then let go of all this
    with no exceptions,
Until you are only light and free.

THE FOG

How to get through the fog of what was
    done or not done.
Of thoughts and emotions,
Imagined fantasies.
Cultural intoxicants,
To be with you
Mind to mind,
Spirit to spirit,
Essence to essence,
Before it is too late.

SO MANY OPINIONS

So many opinions
So many strong ones
About this and that
   and that and this.
Do they reveal the truth?
But then they are never complete,
And sometimes not understandable,
Or get hidden by the words,
Or by belief blindness.
The same with prejudices
   and expectations,
And whatever else our ancestors passed on to us.

So it is best to sit quietly,
Looking deeply
To see into the nature of things,
   their essence,
And the fruits they produce.
Hopefully understanding compassion,
   and not confused unhappiness.

GUIDED TONGLEN MEDITATION

Sit in silence
With calmness
In the place between
Pain and compassion,
Between the in and out breaths.

Then breathe in the pain,
The dark, black, heavy,
Hot, sharp, bitter, searing,
Bone crushing, merciless
Feeling, emotion, thoughts,
Of failure and loss,
Depressive sadness,
Angry rage.

Through every pore and opening
Of your body-mind.

Then breathe it all out
With warm lightness,
Fresh openness,

Spaciousness,
Dancing freedom.

Breathe in the poisons,
The cravings,
Crazy fears,
Stubborn opposition,
Burning attachment.

Through every pore and opening
Of your body-mind.

Then breathe it all out
With loving kindness,
Tender understanding,
Cheerful relief.

STOP TRYING TO BE SOMEBODY

Stop trying to be somebody.
Just be whoever you are,
Mindfully sitting, walking, eating.
Just practice mindful awareness.
Don't be concerned with being someone.
Because you are someone already,
     just as you are.
Who needs to be aware of this.

IMAGINED SELF

Let go of your self-image,
The good, decent, kind, perfect
Teacher, student,
Mentor, meditator,
Group member,
Father, husband,
Mother, wife,
Brother, sister,
Human rights defender,
Worker, citizen,
Retiree, investor,
Car driver, shopper,
Whatever other you have.
They are only imagined,
Delusional fantasies.
Instead
    just be whoever,
    on the Path.

BOWING

How wonderful,
The honor and privilege
To bow
To your teacher,
Loved-one, friend,
Even a stranger
Or enemy.
To the Buddha-to-be within.

With palms together,
As if holding a flower,
Bending toward them,
As you look into their eyes
To their soul
To become one.

ONLY SEE THE FACE BEFORE YOU

To see the face before you,
To only see this face,
And nothing more,
And not to be in a dream,
Or drowning in an ocean
Of thinking thoughts,
Or your rivers of feelings, desires, perceptions.
To see clearly with your senses, ·
The pure awareness of what is
    and nothing more,
This is to be awake
To all the wonders of life,
Until you become them.

It is to see the unclear mind
With its likes and dislikes,
Attachments and aversions,
Analyses and judgments,
Illusions and delusions
Which suffocate awareness.

Just see the face before you,
So you are not tricked and deceived,
Caught and imprisoned.

CALM ABIDING YOGA

As you very slowly stretch
Each body part
While focusing on your breathing,
Starting at your feet and continuing to the top of
your head,
Stretching in every direction,
Breathing each stretch
By observing a breath in and a breath out,
Maybe ten breaths in and then ten out,
Ssooooo slowly each breath-movement,
    in calm abiding.

DO YOU CONTROL YOUR MIND?

Or does your mind control you?
How do you know which?
What about your bodily sensations,
Perceptions, feelings,
And consciousness?
Who's in control?
I only know when I am breathing in,
    I am breathing in.
And when I am breathing out,
    I am breathing out.

ALL PERCEPTIONS ARE INCORRECT

It has taken some time,
To really know how perceptions
Of people, places and things
Are incorrect most often,
    if not all the time.
Looking more deeply than before,
Seeing the constant change in everything,
And the mind-filled dreams and fantasies,
Causes me to wake up

GO BEYOND YOURSELF

Yes, go beyond yourself,
Reach out each day,
To help someone know their mind and feelings,
How to be light and free,
Offer joy to one person in the morning,
And relieve the grief of one person in the
afternoon.
Yes, go beyond yourself
To places you have never been.

BLOCKHEAD

I only know,
I know nothing,
When I am mindful.

For my mind is filled mostly
With useless thoughts
Completely.

"Those who have no thoughts,
Are called Blockheads,"
Said Master Bankei.

Me a mindful blockhead,
How fortunate.

BUMP INTO PEOPLE

Bump into people,
To help them not to mind their business,
So they are light and free.
This is the Way
      to Nirvana.

OUR DREAMS, OUR CHILDREN

We try to have our children live our dreams,
But they find their own,
And how best to live them.
So best to pass the time
Leaving it to the flow.

SO JUST BE

Your hopes and desires,
Your expectations
Bring tension and stress.
There is no peace.
You look for happiness
With old thinking
So it cannot arrive.
You want one thing,
And the world
Gives you something else.
Your present moment wonders
Are taken away.
So just be
With your out-breath.

PERFECT IMPERFECTION

Imperfection is everywhere,
This cannot be denied,
But still you try to be perfect.
Why fight it?
Just be
     imperfectly perfect.

LESS THINKING

How to get your mind,
Not to think so much?
Just ask it a Dharma question,
And listen.

THE FIVE MAGIC SHOWS

I, me, mine fade away,
As I watch the magic shows
Of sensations, feelings, thoughts,
Concepts, and consciousness,
While resting in my original mind.
No more useless thinking, speaking, or acting.

DIFFICULT EMOTIONS

Difficult thought-feelings may arise,
Any moment,
Fear, worry, anxiety,
Regret, anger, condemnation,
Melancholy or panic,
From the endless river of emotions
Each crying out,
To be recognized,
Deeply understood,
Accepted,
Cared for.
The Path,
Which cares for all,
Is the only Way.

ALWAYS FORGIVE

We must forgive everyone
With compassionate understanding,
When their suffering spills on to us,
Their ignorance, criticisms, envy,
Resentments, anger, hatred,
Aggression, hostility,
Egocentric delusions.
And when ours spills out too.
This is the Bodhisattva Way.
Practice the Great Reconciliation Ceremony,
Listen to the nuns and monks of Bat Nha,
Solve the Bat Nha koan,
Until there is oneness.

TEACHING THE DEAD

Caught by their difficulties,
The worldly dharmas,
Their ego's illusory self,
They can't hear you.
You may as well be talking to the dead.

DHARMA SHARING INCANTATION
(Can Use Before Any Dharma Talk or Sharing)

Dear Buddha,
Dear Ancestors,
Dear Teachers,
Dear Thay,
We are grateful you have brought us together
    at this time and place.
Please help us to forget ourselves,
So we may share deeply,
Insight and wisdom about the Dharma,
In the historical and ultimate dimensions.
Please help us discard our inferiority complexes,
Superiority complexes, or equality complexes,
    so there is no duality whatsoever.
I bow to you and
    each Buddha-to-be,
    present here
    in oneness.

EVERY MOMENT PRACTICE

Practice every moment,
Until everything is the Practice,
Yes, you will deeply
    see more
    feel more
    think more
As never before.
Don't be afraid.
Rest in the island of yourself,
To open to great awareness.

FROM WORDS

Words are used by concepts,
To obtain insight,
So there is understanding,
And then wisdom
Giving birth to compassion.

THE [INSERT YOUR NAME HERE] OF YESTERDAY

The [insert your name here] of 5 or 20 years ago
Is not the [insert your name here] of today.
The [insert your name here] of long ago was not
    very understanding,
    compassionate,
    giving,
    joyful.
[Insert your name here] had not found the Path.
Don't judge too harshly.
The same could be said for
    your mother or father,
    grandparents,
Anyone suffering,
They were not themselves.

DON'T LET THEM START

Don't let them start.
Don't let them begin,
Those thoughts,
The usual thoughts.
Catch them quickly!
As they start to arise,
And settle them back down
Into your store consciousness,
So there is no thinking,
Only resting in calm abiding,
And its pure awareness wonders.

DHARMA FLOW

For most of my life
I've not known about the Dharma flow of things,
There was always tension, struggle, difficulties,
   resentments,
But now with empty interbeing,
I go with the flow,
Empty of opinions, beliefs, concepts,
And whatever else I can jettison.

GROUNDED IN GROUNDLESSNESS

Grounded in groundlessness
With its ambiguity and uncertainty,
There is nothing to hold on to,
Because everything is changing.
My empty self goes with the changing flow.

RELIGIONS = DUALITY

Do religions bring duality?
Does duality cause separation?
Is there then us and them?
The chosen and the not chosen?

COMPARISON = 2

Does comparing cause duality?
Does duality cause separation?
Does separation bring favoritism?
And its jealousy and envy?

A MAGIC FORMULA

When you are with the Sangha,
Being held by the Sangha,
Magic happens.
But if you are asleep, you will not see it,
Each sister and brother holding you
In compassionate understanding,
Holding you in unconditional acceptance,
Holding your difficulties
So there is transformation and healing,
Holding your goodness
So it grows and blossoms beyond you,
Holding you in their sisterhood and brotherhood.
And although the magic has no words
It still works its miracles.

I KNOW WHO I AM

I know who I am and do not know.
A student of the Buddha.
Striving and not striving for an open heart-mind.
And with Manas, the self who is in love with
    herself or himself
    in calm abiding,
We are with the 10,000 things,
And this sindhu on my wrist continues to remind
me.

WHEN ANGER APPEARS

When anger appears,
Do not say anything,
Do not do anything.
Just breathe in and breathe out
With one hundred percent concentration.
Anger comes and goes,
As all Dharma phenomena.
Often disguised
As irritation, resentments,
And other dissatisfactions,
When people and things
Are not the way we want them.
Breathing in, I know I am breathing in.
Breathing out, I know I am breathing out.
I let go of anger.

THEY HAVE NOT SPOKEN TO PROVOKE YOU

They have not spoken to provoke you.
Their words slipping out of mindless minds.
Robots speaking ego manifestations.
Do nothing.
Say nothing.
And you remain in the Pure Land.

SO MANY DEMONS AND HELLS

Possibly with the next thought,
A demon or hell,
A hair's breadth away.
Greed, hatred, ignorance,
Secret police, soldiers, prison, death,
Be alert!

RIP OUT EVERYTHING

Everything must be ripped out of your mind,
All conditioning propaganda,
Notions, opinions, beliefs,
Advertisements,
Teachings,
If you want freedom.

TEA IN THE AFTERNOON

Afternoon tea
With my mother,
When I was a boy
After school.
We'd talk
About life
Of a son, a child.
Hot Lipton tea
With milk
And sugar.
A New England sun
Shining warm,
Outside and inside.
How wonderful.
Even this memory.

SOME POEMS CAN BE KOANS

An arrow shot into your mind.
You wonder day and night,
Struggling to pull it out,
Knowing it needs a visceral
    mind-body answer.
So don't think.

KOANS

Wherever we find ourselves.
Whoever we find ourselves with.
Whatever is in front of us,
That which we are dealing with today,
At this time and place,
Day after day,
Is our Practice on the Path.
Each is a koan,
A Zen meditation riddle.
Unsolved, unsettled,
Lodged into us.
Not to be solved intellectually,
But with mindful awareness,
And one-point focused concentration.
Not a misfortune.
But an opportunity to penetrate deeply
And answer life's great questions.
So there is no more fear
    or questioning.
Only calm abiding in the moment
    with what is.

REST YOUR MIND

Rest your mind at your hara
Just below your navel.
This is a doorway to a wondrous world,
Always in front of you,
But blocked by your thoughts.
It is where you are with your whole being,
Your unborn Buddha mind,
Your Buddha nature,
The Ultimate Dimension.
Try it!
Open the door!
Enter!
But do not waver
Or enlightenment will be lost.

MOTHER'S DAY

I am aware of my mother,
Grandmothers, great grandmothers,
   in me.
All my blood ancestral mothers,
Spiritual ancestral mothers,
Neighborhood and community mothers,
Of the many motherly instincts,
Kindness, tenderness, and love,
Passed on to live in me.
Happy Mother's Day
To all of them.

DON'T TRY SO HARD

Don't try so hard
   to be
Whatever,
Rich, powerful,
A doctor, lawyer,
Wall Street executive,
Artist, athlete,
Or some other form.
Just be nobody
   not doing.
So you can rest
In your Buddha nature.
Then you will really be
   some body
   some one.

IT'S ALL ABOUT WAKING UP

It's all about waking up.
Being awake all the time,
Whenever you think or speak,
Wherever you are,
Whatever you are doing.
Meditation is being awake.
Walking mindfully is being awake.
When asked: "Who or what are you?"
The Buddha answered: "I am awake."
Your unborn Buddha mind is a mind that is awake.
Being awake means to wake up from a dream,
So you are fully present right here and now,
Not lost in thoughts,
In doing,
In becoming.
But being with this in-breath,
And this out-breath.

EGONESS AT ITS FINEST

I'm going to teach other car drivers
How to drive correctly
By getting aggressively close to them.
To teach my wife, husband, partner, child
How to think and act correctly
By constantly telling them what,
And what not to do.
The same with our politicians,
Our country's leaders and others.
The little king or queen reigns supreme.
Egoness at its finest,
Needs mindful care,
Lest it believe it is real.

HOW'S YOUR EGO?

How's your ego?
That sense of me and mine,
It's not yours, his, hers, or theirs.
Understanding such infantile infatuations,
Helps you to be alive
In the real world.

PLEASE FORGIVE THE EGOISM

Please forgive the egoism
With its egotistical thinking, feeling, speaking, and
   acting,
Its sly cunning ruthless aggression
   to have it his way.
Please excuse this frightened beast
Who loves himself so much,
He becomes blind and heartless.
Please have mercy
And help him find the Way
   to the Buddha, Dharma and Sangha.

EGO MIND

Born with the unborn Buddha mind,
And with Buddha nature,
The mind is immense.
It can hold all phenomena.

Born with the ego mind,
and its ego nature,
The mind is small.
It holds very little.

From cultural conditioning
Egocentricity reigns.
If you want emancipation,
Drink the Dharma deeply.

IS THIS THOUGHT USEFUL?

Ask yourself all the time:
"Is this thought useful?"
Useful for my emancipation and freedom,
To be light and free
In calm abiding in the present moment?

Be relentless.
Let no unwholesome thought,
Feeling, sensation, perception or
State of consciousness escape this question.
This is your mantra every moment,
Your daily koan.

Part 2
Is this thought useful to whoever you meet,
Speak to?
Useful for their emancipation and freedom?
Be relentless.

WHY IS BOWING SO IMPORTANT?

Because it is an effective efficient way
To dissolve the ego king or queen Manas,
Right away quickly,
And her romantic delusions
About self love
Into emptiness.

A STUDENT

2 weeks free,
singer,
piano, keyboard player,
6 feet 4 inches
flip flops
short pants.
I search inside for my essence,
beyond egocentricity,
the grasping,
craving,
the dysfunctioning,
in and around me.
It is there.
Calm abiding.
Just need to stop and look.
This is where I belong.
Even in the madness.
So I can help them too
To be emancipated,
To be free,
To be freedom.
Transformation and healing,
Always just one mindful breath away.

So simple.

HOW DO YOU FACE YOURSELF ALONE?

How do you face yourself?
First, be alone completely
With no distractions,
Like when sitting in meditation.
And see what presents itself.
Petty concerns and interests.
Egocentric ones.
Fears, regrets, worries,
Greed, hatred, delusions.
That things are not the way you want them.
You and others are not either.
Don't stop there.
Look deeply until you understand
Their empty oneness.
Aloneness is just a tool
To penetrate deeply into what is.

A MAD WORLD

Do we live in a mad world?
Yes, there is much anger and hatred,
Greed and delusion everywhere.
These three poisons are in us,
Which the entertainment, and
Infotainment, and
Newstainment media
Cultivate and glorify.
Such that the very path to suffering
Is said to be the path to enlightenment,
And happiness.
Is this not madness?

ARE WE ALL ADDICTS?

Are we all addicts;
Do we swim in a sea of addictions,
And thus by osmosis
Take in some kind of them.
Maybe to food, TV, alcohol, drugs,
Celebrity-ism, money, power,
Violence, sex,
Ignorance, prejudice,
Beliefs, notions, delusions?

How then not to drown?
Breathe in mindfully fully one-hundred percent,
Do the same as you breathe out.

WHY SO NEGATIVE?

Have you noticed
How negative your mind
Can be often.
You might need to watch it closely
To catch these thoughts.
They can hide in the background.
But you'll see them with practice
Of looking deeply.
See them ready to undermine
Your peace and tranquility.
Your enlightened nirvana.
Where do they come from?
Why are they here?
Family and social conditioning
For survival,
Or from the three poisons.
What then to best handle them?
Keep looking deeply.
Go through to the other side.

THE DHARMA SHOWS NO DISTINCTIONS

The Dharma shows no distinctions
For class, status, role,
Occupation, family,
Or what have you.
It protects, heals, and enlightens
Anyone who drinks it in.
A medicine!
No?

HOW TO TEST FOR EGOCENTRICITY?

To know how egocentric you are
(or others),
Simply drive a car,
And look at your driving
Reactions, thoughts, feelings,
Perceptions, and consciousness.
How's your driving?
The other drivers?
Competition, aggression,
Get-out-of-my-way, or
Helping others get safely
    to their destination?

WHAT DO YOU LABEL YOURSELF

What do you label yourself
In the morning, afternoon, and evening?
Look carefully
As the mind labels quickly,
Superior, inferior, equal.
Attractive or not so much,
Young, old, sick, healthy.
Greedy, generous.
Industrious, lazy.
Why the labeling
Moment to moment without end.
Can you be unlabeled?
To just be you.
What about your labeling others?

ANOTHER TRUTH

Just realized the truth:
That I will never get it all together.
And as I grow older,
That everything is falling apart!
Such is the way of the Dharma.

MINDFULNESS BELLS DURING FIRST RETREAT

His mannerisms are disturbing me.
Why doesn't she act like an adult.
That was a negative remark.
Look how chummy he is.
Look how he puts his hands.
She's always complaining.
Notice how he is always late.
She told me to be silent or move elsewhere.
Why does he have to sit in front of me.
She doesn't practice smiling much.
All these announcements.
And those professionals---
Is it smugness?
Are they talking about me?
Here comes another bow that I'm not ready for.
At least it was not a smile.
Sometimes I find these mindfulness bells too mindful.
Don't you?

MONKS OR NUNS AT FIRST PLUM VILLAGE RETREAT

Noticed the two shining globes.
Two worlds sacred simplicity
Of non-attachment.
Monks or Nuns?
I don't know.
But their majestic stillness,
Came inside me.
As I sat in back of their shaved heads.
Hopeful they will take me
With them
    to nirvana.

CAN YOU STEAL EMPTINESS?

What do these Monks and Nuns have.
These smiling, bowing centers of calmness.
These rebels against ignorance,
Who want to transform themselves and me
Into agents of loving-kindness.

Can they give it to me as a present?
Or can I steal it?
Can you steal emptiness?
Can you put your hands around no-self?
Can inter-being be put in a bag and carried away?

WHAT IS THE DHARMA?

What is the Dharma?
The teachings of the Buddha,
About true reality.
The Four Noble Truths,
And the Eight Fold Path.

The Dharma is everything.

WHEN ON THE ROAD DRIVING DO NOT GET SUCKED IN
(Place this on your dashboard)

When on the road driving your car,
Do not get sucked into their pushing
Aggression, lack of civil politeness.
Do not be contaminated
By their egocentric violence
(Or yours).
Stay clear
In calm abiding.
This is the Way.

THE LIVING DEAD

Have you ever noticed
When you are talking
With a loved one, friend, neighbor,
Acquaintance, or store clerk
They are already speaking on top of your words or
thoughts,
As if you are not there.
Watching TV, listening to the radio,
Typing into their computer or video game,
Smart cell phone.
Lost in their devices,
Worries, regrets, fears,
Ambitions,
Multitasking.
The living dead?
How to help them wake up.
Breathe in,
Breathe out.

THE HOUSE

Yes, a house can be a home,
And a home a house.
But a house is also like a lover
Very demanding and expensive.
Wanting things the way we want them
Can never be,
Because this is like that
And that is like this.
Perfectionism brings difficulties.
So it is always better to go with the flow
Of deep understanding.
Who are you?
What is really important?
The sound of the birds?
The swaying of the trees?
Knowing completely
You are breathing this breath in
And the next out.
There are so many wonders
Needing our attention.

HOW TO REMEMBER

The mind is always forgetting.
You try to remember
To be mindful,
But it forgets.
And forgets better
As you get older.
When it does remember
Often it's an unpleasant
Regret, fear,
Gain or loss.
Or not being treated as you wish.
How many books have you read?
What did they have to say?
It's the same with lectures and conversations.
Maybe its nature is to forget,
To let go,
Not to be attached,
So it can bring you to the land of calm abiding.

PLUMS

Are plums like prunes?
Can they loosen attachments?
Can they take away desires?
If the answers are yes,
Imagine living in a Plum Village.
You could sit and let things pass.
You could be empty of your self.
You could be free of so much crap.

~or this one~

PLUMS

Are plums a laxative,
Like prunes are?
If they are, what can they loosen up?
What can they take away?
Can they loosen attachments?
Take away desires?
If yes,
Imagine living in a Plum Village.
You could sit and let things pass.
And be empty of your self.
You could be free.

SILENCE

Can you be comfortable with silence?
With the comfort it brings?
With the rest it gives the mouth and mind?

So much speech seems mindless.
Constant chatter to drown out the self.
With its suffering and non-suffering.

Can you be comfortable with no words?
Without the pain or joy they bring?
Without the habit to talk?

Be with me silently,
So we can talk another way.

MI AMOR

When the planning stops,
When the remembering ends,
When the thinking does not start,
Metta unfolds.

A NEW BEGINNING

To start each day
With beginner's mind
Empty of last night's nightmares,
Without tomorrow's dreams---
No tides of conceiving.
The happy sage
Is one with an empty mind.

BEGINNING ANEW

Please let me tell you
About a hurtful word or behavior
You have given me.
It made me so sad.
I tell you so resentment
Will not take root.
So anger will not be planted.
So separation will not set in.
So tenderness will not be ended.
So sweetness will not be replaced.
So love will not be lessened.
Please listen to me
Without a response
Without defenses
Without interruptions.
Let it rest for five days
Then tell me what you think,
What you feel.
I will listen.
I will listen mindfully.

Please let me tell you
About a wonderful word or behavior

You have given me.
It made me so happy.
I tell you so love grows.
So tenderness is furthered.
So sweetness is deepened.
So joy is nurtured.
So happiness is shared.
Please listen to me.
Without interruptions.
Let it rest for five days.
Then tell me what you think.
What you feel.
I will listen.
I will listen mindfully.

THOUGHTS

What are they thinking about?
Are they caught in their thoughts
About how others are thinking about them?
And if others are thinking thoughts
About others thinking thoughts about them,
And if I am thinking thoughts
About others thinking thoughts about me,
Then we are lost in our thoughts,
And not here for each other.

WALKING MEDITATION FOR THEM

So loving, calming, nourishing,
Connecting intimately with Mother Earth
With each step,
As her healing life force
Flows up into me.
I walk like this.

For all those living in hell,
Hungry, abused, robbed, raped,
Vilified, falsely convicted,
Imprisoned, silenced, hidden,
I walk like this.

(Now the hard part)
And for those who inflict this suffering,
In one way or another.
I walk like this.

A WORKER'S MORNING

"I love you," he yells.
As he backs his car out of the driveway.
She in pajamas standing with pointed finger, yells
back,
"No live wires."
"No drinking on the job."
A wife-mother's voice
To this worker
Leaving for the job.

EVALUATION FEAR HABIT ENERGY

Evaluation fear habit energy,
From automatic, instantaneous
Self-evaluations in every moment
By parents, teachers, friends, and numerous
beings,
To be and do it their way,
Better or not at all,
At least not how you are.
The best response?
Breathe in.
Breathe out.

EVERYONE IS YOU

Your son or daughter is you.
Spouse, neighbor too.
There is no one who is not you.
"Love thy neighbor as thyself," said Jesus.
Be kind to yourself.

MELDING WITH THE EARTH

As each foot touches
The ground, asphalt, cement, wooden floor,
Grass or earth,
My shoes and feet
Meld with Mother Earth,
Her cleansing, healing elements
Flowing into my body-mind,
A continuous energy of oneness.
This is walking meditation.

HARSH AGGRESSIVE THOUGHTS AND WORDS

When harsh aggressive thoughts or words are present
There is violence in you or others,
You have become them
With all their destruction.
So think and speak the opposite.

ON-RETREAT

Why not be on-retreat all the time?
Whether walking, standing, sitting, eating,
defecating,
With full awareness and concentration.
In silence looking deeply
Into the miracles before you,
A blade of grass, the wind, sunshine, drops of rain,
Your mindful breath.
As they arise and pass away
While calmly abiding
In oneness.

JUDGING JUDGMENT

Such a heavy affliction.
Teachers tell us to beware of the judging mind.
We all have one,
Negatively commenting instantaneously,
Passed on from our ancestors
    and the culture we live in,
Watered so frequently by so many,
It can have us give up the most precious of all gifts:
    the Dharma,
If we are not careful.

INFERIOR ME

Where does the poor self come from?
What are its material parts?
A wounded child or older person,
Demands of family, job, culture
To be a particular way,
This constant self-evaluation,
Causing self-consciousness,
So the authentic self is murdered.
Know yourself to forget yourself
So you can be one with everything.

DRINKING IN THROUGH ALL MY SENSES

Drinking in through all my senses
This mountain's vista
Enters me.
It is the same with this blue sky
And white clouds.
Such intoxicating wondrous oneness
Can make you drunk with aliveness!

THERE ARE NO BIG DEALS

There are no big deals
So why bother.
Bow equally to every situation.
It's no big deal.

TRYING TO MAKE SENSE?

It's all about trying to make some sense of it.
To figure it out, to understand.
Who am I?
What is my purpose?
What is the best way?
Society gives us the worldly Dharma.
Fame, fortune, pleasure, your way.
Religions create various answers.
The most fortunate find the Dharma.

IMPERFECT

Everything and everyone is imperfect,
Including you,
Because they are not the way you want them, or
How others want them.
But is your way or theirs correct?
And too everything contains unsatisfactoriness,
Everything, nothing is exempt.
Thus, there is nothing wrong with imperfection.
Because that is how things are.
But if you look deeply
You will find perfection in imperfection,
And bliss will follow.

TAKE GOOD CARE OF THE OLD PERSON IN YOU

We all have an old person in us.
Just like we have a wounded child.
That part of us not understood,
Treated badly,
Or violently without love.
Who needs to be understood,
Protected,
To hear she is accepted
Unconditionally just as she is
With all his limitations,
Confusions,
Defects and failures.
Tell him right now
That everything is okay,
That you will protect him,
Care for and love her
Just as she is.

YES, HOLD IT ALL

Exclude Nothing,
Your idiosyncratic habit energies, mind stories,
thinking,
That make you suffer,
Your fears, regrets, anxieties, doubts,
Should have done,
Didn't do it correctly,
The judging criticisms of yourself and others.
You can add to this:
Sickness, body falling apart,
Fear of death,
Of dying alone,
The ignorance, greed, and hatred throughout the
world.
Yes, hold them with your compassionate heart,
With no expectations, no doing it right.
Just hold them all,
Loosely,
As they arise and pass away.

AN ARTIST

Always wanted to be an artist,
Tried to be one.
Then learned: art is everything,
It is everywhere,
We are all artists.
Add mindfulness
    and it goes deep
    without boundaries.

DON'T SPACE OUT

Please don't space out.
You know that place of bliss,
When you stop and breathe in and out,
Fully aware of your breath, body and mind.
Don't stay there.
When you can travel to places
Beyond thoughts, feelings, sensations,
Perceptions and states of consciousness,
Beyond your dreams,
Where you understand
The very nature of yourself,
Others and all phenomena,
Becoming one with them
    living an awakened life.

WHY BEING WITH MONASTICS IS SO IMPORTANT

They practice mindfulness 24/7,
Drinking the energy of Dharma teachings,
From the essence of a long line of teachers
Going all the way back to the Buddha,
Embodying his Sangha and those that followed,
Living for us to know and love the Dharma
So we are free of our suffering.
Does this not make sense then,
To be with them as much as possible?
Or others like them.

PRACTICING MINDFULNESS ALL THE TIME

How the world is depends on how you wake up in
the morning,
And brush your teeth,
How and What you eat for breakfast.
Don't tell me you are too busy.
Look at your resisting habit energies excuses.
Everything you do can be done mindfully,
Done beautifully.
There is nothing you cannot be mindful about.
So there is no reason for you
Not to be practicing mindfulness all the time.

DON'T SAY YOU DON'T HAVE TIME

So you say you don't have time for mindful living,
Which can make you free, joyful and happy.
That you are too busy with busyness.
This is not true,
Because when you get up in the morning and
brush your teeth,
Urinate, get dressed, drink some tea, drive to work,
and so on,
They can be done mindfully.
Thus everything can be with full aware
concentration,
And when this happens you are a Buddha.

BE QUICK!

Be quick!
To see how your mind in a flash
Even before your eyes open in the morning
Goes to negative evaluations, opinions, beliefs,
notions,
Based on your family social schooling,
Maybe survival instincts too.
But know simultaneously this kind of thinking is
not helpful for liberation,
As it fills you with the poisons of fear, worry, low
self-esteem,
When instead you can drink in
Hope, joy, confidence, understanding, kindness.

WHEN SHOULD SUFFERING BE PUT ASIDE?

After you have talked about it
With yourself or others,
Have looked into its root causes and conditions,
Have seen its nature,
Then put it to rest.
Not that it will not cry out again,
Wanting to be taken care of.
But you again a concerned mother
Will do what is necessary to care for his fear and
worry
So he can rest calmly
    until he falls asleep.

DO I HAVE THIS CORRECT?

The fires of greed, hatred, and ignorance
Are raging in many parts of the world
Such that people are constantly being
Murdered, raped, tortured, falsely imprisoned,
Starved, beaten, robbed,
And in other ways forced to live in hells,
And you mass media are telling me
That some trivial thing happened or did not
happen
With this entertainer or politicians or whoever,
Or some other insignificant event took place,
And they are more important concerns?
I just don't get it.
Please help me understand.

MAKE A LIST OF YOUR ATTACHMENTS

I'm attached to:
My body, looks, appearance,
Certain negative thoughts, feelings,
perceptions, sensations,
Could be pleasant ones too,
My children, partner,
Good health, certain foods,
Creature comforts,
My house, apartment, car, clothes, computer,
Having things my way,
And so on.
Deep looking and shining light eyes
Will add your hidden attachments.
List them in priority order.
Now you have the causes of your suffering.

GREAT VIOLENCE ALL AROUND US

Yes, there is great violent thinking and actions
By our government officials and that of others.
Presidents, legislators, CIAs, generals, police,
The media, and others working with them,
Which kill, murder, falsely imprison, torture,
Falsely convict, maim, cripple,
With great cruelty, brutality, and inhumanness,
Which destroys minds, bodies, and the property of
millions.
Hidden, suppressed, denied, not heard or seen,
So they can keep their power or get more,
Their good jobs, careers, bank accounts,
Retirement income, house, car, comfortable
security,
Marriage, esteemed status, acceptance,
So they are not shunned, ostracized, banned,
imprisoned.
What is one to do?
Breathe in,
Breathe out.
Rest in calm abiding,
To find your answer.

WHAT'S AT YOUR CUTTING EDGE

To go where no one has gone before
Is to be at the cutting edge of our practice,
Our spiritual development.
But here at the frontier
You can expect resistance, Uncomfortableness
Maybe fear, anxiety
About the new growth and expansion toward
liberation.
So get anchored in your breath.

NO-MAN'S LAND

No-man's land
With its paradoxes
Ambiguity
Uncertainty
Helplessness
Impermanent change
Emptiness.
No control---
　Even of my thoughts
This is the Way
So be kind
To yourself
And others
Without exception.

CALL ON YOUR ANCESTORS FOR HELP

Yes, call on your blood and spiritual ancestors
For their guidance and help.
They are there inside of you,
With their wanting to protect and care for you,
With deep loving kindness and love.
Wishing you only the best in your life.
For you are their continuation.
You are them.
Call to your ancestors.

THE BUDDHADHARMA WORLD

Your Practice Is
Your practice location
or meditation hall is wherever
You find yourself,
At home, in a car, an office, shopping,
With whoever you are with
Loved one, friend, those you dislike,
Whoever is pushing your buttons.

HOW MANY DHARMA BOOKS AND TALKS?

How many books have you read,
Reports, magazines,
TV programs and films taken in,
Dharma talks listened to?
What did you learn?
What stayed with you?
Interesting how little the mind remembers.
Maybe that's why daily practice,
Attending as many retreats as possible,
As well as Dharma talks is so important.

STOPPING PRACTICE

Maybe the most important practice is stopping.
Say nothing.
Do nothing.
Just sit there
In calm abiding,
Breathing in and breathing out.
From this arises the wisdom
To act like a Buddha.

THE GOLFERS

Retired or not retired
To southern states
They play golf or tennis each day
With their golfing tennis friends
Hitting a ball here then there,
While the fires of samsara burn Night and Day
Causing endless suffering everywhere
Does this make sense?

ON THE CUSHION MEDITATION

There is "on the cushion practice"
And "off the cushion,"
Just as there are "engaged Buddhism"
And "temple Buddhism."
Which one are you?

BE MY SECOND BODY

Will you be my second body,
And could I be your second body,
So we can practice as Bodhisattvas.
We all need someone
To know how well we are
Taking good care of our struggles,
Aspirations and joys.
How wonderful to have someone
Who cares as if you were each other.

NO SPECIAL ROBE

There is no special robe or coat
That needs to be put on.
To be carried,
To be tailored,
There is only being with the flow,
Resting in the unborn Buddha Mind.

THE PRIME DIRECTIVE

So it seems the prime directive
Of mind-body,
Are my should's, ought to be's,
Those internal voices of my parents, ancestors,
My socially conditioned fabricated self,
Who wants things his way,
The way things ought to be.
This is habit energy.
The only way to handle it,
Is to know when I am breathing-in,
I know I am breathing-in,
And when breathing-out,
I know I am breathing-out.
This is the key.

WHAT TO DO WITH AN ANGRY
ENRAGED LOVED ONE

Say nothing,
Do nothing,
Be with your breath
As you breathe in and breathe out,
One hundred percent.
Take a mindful walk.
Notice all your impulsive thoughts and feelings,
And let them all go,
Including those about telling him off,
Putting them in their place,
Pointing out their wrongnesses.
Of course do not permit any physical violence to you
or others,
Leave, move out, go to a shelter if necessary.
Accept them with their hatred, greed and ignorance.
Accept this broken egocentric human,
With the causes and conditions
That have manifested before you.
And from this place practice the Dharma
As deeply as possible
To help them wake up
To who they are and what they are doing.
This is not an easy koan.

A SHAKER, A MAKER

Maybe not a shaker or a maker,
But a simple practitioner of the Way,
Knowing only,
When I breathe in I know I am breathing in.
The same with breathing out,
As each foot touches the ground,
While walking the Path.
That is all that is.

WHEN A LOVED ONE IS SICK
September 25, 2006, Sarasota, Florida

When a loved one is sick,
With some kind of illness,
And they might die,
We tolerate and forgive,
Their unkindness, forgetfulness,
Ignorance, egotism, pride;
All their delusions.

Then what do things matter now
While they are alive with us?

AFFLICTIVE EMOTIONS (KLESHAS)
February 19, 2015 (five months before Bill passed away)
Longboat Key, Florida

Let's say you have an afflictive emotion,
Could be fear, worry, anxiety, regret,
Anger, resentment,
Negative judging, criticizing,
Self-condemnation, or condemning others or a
situation.

You know, those painful places you find yourself in.
What are you to do?
First, stop right where you are,
And say to yourself: "That's okay."
Keep repeating this mantra: "That's okay."
Accept the negative thoughts,
The emotional pain,
Because it is what is.

Next realize that it's just a thought, a feeling.
Therefore, a fleeting passing unsubstantial condition,
"Like a tiny drop of dew, or a bubble floating in a
stream;
Like a flash of lightning in a summer cloud,

Or a flickering lamp, an illusion, a phantom, or a
dream."*

Then focus completely on your breathing in and
breathing out.
Let your breath embrace, caress, take care of you.
Then wish that you, the other person, the situation,
To be well, happy, peaceful, calm, smiling,
Healthy, safe, unharmed.

Then take a walk with full awareness of your feet
Gently touching the ground.
Notice the wonders around you,
Like your walking, your seeing, Mother Earth,
A flower, the blue sky, your breathing.

Recall some wonderful happy refreshing moments,
Like being with nature, looking at the stars,
Being with a loved one, a good friend,
Having a good cup of tea, a piece of pizza.
Do all of this for those who are not able to.

(from the Diamond Sutra)

STAGE FOUR LUNG CANCER
April 5, 2015(three months before Bill passed away)
Longboat Key, Florida

With the diagnosis
Stage four lung cancer,
The life I knew is gone.
The Bill I knew is not here anymore.
My conditioned fabricated separate self,
All his petty egocentric delusions.
The way I did things, thought about things, gone.
My way of being with family, friends, others, gone.
The certainty of things, gone.
My body as I knew it, gone.
My way of living, gone.
Only impermanent impermanence,
Interdependent interbeingness are here,
In this wonderful present moment,
With the Three Jewels (the Buddha, Dharma, and
Sangha),
Which keep me solid and stable.
What more can one want?

THANK YOU CANCER AND PAIN

Thank you Cancer,
Thank you Pain,
You saved my life,
You gave me unbelievable Dharma teachings,
To see clearly the real truths of life,
To understand what is most important,
And have allowed me to bring this to others,
That could not have been possible otherwise.
I bow to you my dear friends,
As I do to the Buddhas, Bodhisattvas, Great
Masters.
Namaste.

CANCER SHOCK

The shock of the cancer diagnosis
Was quite something!
A lifetime of doing things this way,
Mine or someone else's to some extent,
Changed, just like that.
Impermanence appeared upright and stable,
Direct experience it is called.
Zen at its finest.
I bow to impermanence,
I bow to direct experience,
I bow to living our so-called "regular life."
With family, job,
Dharma living.
Namaste.

FRAGILE LIFE

Life is very fragile,
Limited.
Death is near,
Hovering about,
Or sickness.
We are together briefly.
What then is the worth of any possession,
Fame, power.
Or being with a son, daughter,
Loved one or good friend,
Today in this present moment,
To savor,
Right now.

TIME'S RUNNING OUT

Time's running out,
Death waits around every corner,
Particularly for the old ones,
As the natural flow continues.
Thus stopping and breathing,
Having a cup of tea in the afternoon
So important.
Just be still to enjoy being,
Before it's too late!

DEATH

Death is simply mother Earth calling you
    back to your true home,
Which we forget because of our thinking,
That's why each foot step
Needs to be soft and loving.

DEATH AND LIFE

When young,
Like those now,
You spoke of life and death
As not important,
Like they are doing.

But in the shank of life,
All tastes sweet,
Each breath and step,
Sunrise and flower,
Divine.

We hold on
No matter.
Enjoying,
The sweetness.

HOW TO BE WITH THE DYING OR DEAD

How am I to be With the dying?
With the living dead?
With the dead?

To be with them,
Be with them
As you would be with yourself,
In the present moment,
With this out-breath.

With an empty self
Open to all things,
Connected to all things,
Intimately with the oneness
Of life and death.

THERE IS NO DEATH OR BIRTH

Death visits often,
Sometimes suddenly
Sometimes over time.
We are of the nature to die.
We will die.
Death is life.
Life is death.

As the rain travels to the river,
And the river to the ocean,
And the ocean to the rain clouds.
All is one, one is all.

There is no birth;
There is no death.
Only letting go
Back into this sea
Of constant change.

WHY CAN'T DEATH BE APPRECIATED?

Why can't death be appreciated,
Just like life is.
Is it not just another mind-body state,
That arises and passes away?

Epilogue

Learn to be present to whatever arises,
To whatever is in front of you.
Without the drama, grasping, attachment, endless
rumination.
Without your story line,
I am a busy person. Judging person.
An aggressive person. Type A.
A what's-in-it-for-me person.
Or a poor-me helpless victim,
A person wanting this, not wanting that.
Listen to the language words.
Look at how you frame things.
At what you project out onto others, the world.
How you get stuck in your stories and projections,
Believing them to be real.
Thus causing yourself and others much suffering.
Leave the world of ego fantasies,
And live in the Buddhadharma world
Where you stop and look into the nature of all
things,
Into the nature of your mind,
In order to understand them deeply,
Which will liberate and set you free
From all afflictions.
(Help others to do the same.)

—*William P. Menza*

Acknowledgements

William P. Menza wished to thank and acknowledge the following teachers, friends and loved ones who walked together with him in the "Dharma Rain" and so, in one way or another, in small ways and large, helped birth these poems and bring this compilation to completion:

Venerable Thich Nhat Hanh.

The staff and friends at The Whole Salamander Publishing Collective, especially Beth DeLap and Ken Lenington, and including Sandy Garcia, for their solid and stable steadfastness in organizing and getting this book together for publication. Without them this book would not be.

My wife Alicia (a hidden Bodhisattva), my son Charles, my grandson Oliver. My mother and father, Louise N. Menza and William V. Menza.

My brothers and sisters: Charles Menza, my twin brother, deceased 2015. Joan Menza, now Sister Naomi at St. Patrick's church in Boston. Louise Menza Henderson, deceased 2014. Pamela Menza Veysey, James Menza.

Dr. Elliot Dasher, with Kaiser Permanente HMO, who taught stress reduction and sent me to the Barre Insight Meditation Center for a week to learn to meditate. I changed.

All the monks and nuns at Blue Cliff Monastery and Deer Park Monastery.

Dharma teachers Anh Huong Nguyen and Thu Nguyen of my root sangha The Fairfax Mindfulness Center of Fairfax, VA; its members, and especially their Order of Interbeing (OI) members Garrett Phelan and Jane Phelan.

Members of the River and Mountains Sangha in Putney, Vermont, and Dharma teacher Richard Brady, my 30 years mentor and friend, his wife, OI member and mentor Elisabeth Dearborn.

Still Water Practice Center, Takoma Park, Maryland, especially Dharma teacher Mitchell Ratner, and its OI and long-term members: Joann Malone and Pat Smith, Susan Hadler, Scott Schang, Julia Jarvis, Valerie Stains, Jindra Cekan, Brigitte Pichot, who also practice with the Washington Community of Mindfulness and the Mindfulness Practice Center of Fairfax, Virginia.

Dharma teachers Rowan Conrad of Frenchtown, Montana; Jack Lawlor of Evanston, IL; Al Lingo of Decatur, GA; Ernestine Enomoto of Honolulu, HI; Joanne Friday and her husband Robert of Matunuck,

RI; Leslie Rawls of Charlotte, NC; Lyn Fine of Berkeley, CA; and Marjorie Markus of New York, NY.

Bruce Nichols and Judith Stevens, longtime Order of Interbeing members and friends in CT; and now Garette and Jane Phelan who have moved to CT.

Diane Strausser in Columbus, Ohio.

Boston Old Path Sangha Dharma teacher Elizabeth Wood, members of the sangha and OI members, particularly members and friends Joan Kimball and Avi Magidoff.

The Washington Community of Mindfulness, my root sangha, and its solid members, such as Steve Sidley, and many who have moved on to other communities, like Jim and Freddie Schrider in Portland, Oregon, and my good friend Carole Baker.

Members of the Boat of Compassion Sangha, Fairfax, VA, my root sangha, especially Dharma teachers Vien Van Nguyen and Que Kim Tran.

Members of the Lido Zendo, Lido Beach, Florida, especially Estelle Gerard who built the Zendo at her home and maintained a solid and stable sitting group and Day of Mindfulness; and its steadfast members Fran Kaplan, Ed Hurley, Bill Morgan, Ishmael Katz, and Dorothy Conlon (deceased).

Members of the Derbyshire Farm Meditation Group in Wilton, NH; especially Bruce Kanter who organized the group year after year and sold his farm to Temple Forest Monks.

The Ledgewood Condo Discussion Meditation Group, Milford, NH, who continue sitting and discussing the Dharma even though I cannot be with this new group.

Members of the Morning Sun Mindfulness Practice Center, Alstead, NH, especially Dharma teacher Br. Michael Ciborski and Dharma teacher Sister Fern Dorresteyn who built this intentional community and facilitate its many activities and developments.

The Community of Mindful Living in the Pines, founded and facilitated by Emily Whittle and John Bowan (who are caregivers for Emily's 97-years-old parents). This was my refuge over the years as I snowbirded North or South, and when I was not using the Auto-Train (which was like being on retreat). The Dharma discussions so wonderful. They meet at the Congregational Church of Pinehurst, North Carolina.

Our 709 Sitting Group was most wonderful with its solid and stable practitioners Robin Ingles, Phil Travers, Susan Kyle, Fred Burgraf, John Clements, Marilyn Martin, Catherine Sedney and Winnie Montgomery. The group started about 1989 and continues in Susan's home when possible. It was called 709 because that was the conference room that was always available at lunchtime. We would sit for about 20 minutes and end with a discussion on a topic someone initiated. One sitting was on how to eat a Krispy Kreme doughnut. Fred used his weight reduction program to show how to eat mindfully. We sat weekly until about 1996 when Robin suggested we meet Monday to Friday. And so we sat each day of the week we were at the office. We had some non-agency practitioners sit with us also until security became too difficult to allow them into the building.

A special acknowledgement to the Florida Community of Mindfulness OI members, OI aspirants, and those who want to be an OI member. I thank each of you for being who you are and for what you have given me to be who I am. I could not know and live the Dharma without your wonderful help and support. Thank you.

Florida Community of Mindfulness Dharma Teacher Fred Eppsteiner. OI members, Aspirants, and longtime practitioners: Angela Parrish, Ruth Fishel, Sam Warlick, Marilyn Warlick, John Daugirda, Viviann Plenge, Rosaria Pugliese, Andrew Rock, Chris Bush, Nancy Natilson, Mary Duncan, Darlene Stewart, Anne Kracmer, Elena Rigg, Ken Lenington, Antonio Brunner, Barbara Hawk, Jacqulyn Schuett, Charlie Stewart, Bill Lee, Bryan

Hindert, Steve Geisz, Christina Walker, Robert Lassiter, Betsy Arizu, Alex Lerner, Diane Powell, Salima Grannon, Chip Burson, Emmet Bondurant, Andrew Solis, Steve Bowling, Robbie Ross Tisch, Martina McNaboe.

Special thanks to Bruce Kantner who maintained the Derbyshire Wednesday Sitting Group over the past 3 or 4 years. Bruce is the director of the GAIA Education Outreach Institute. Sitting would be Bruce, his wife Barbara, Will Moylan, Ken Davis, Judy Gross, and Jackie Davis. Sitting at Derbyshire Farm was a special treat as we met in a small building in a large forested farm. Bruce sold his property to Forest Monks from England and Thailand. The monks were invited to eat their meal for the day each Sunday and held a Day of Mindfulness now and then. An interesting tradition as they cannot touch money, they wear only the robe of a monk with sandals like in the days of the Buddha and must beg each day for their one meal eaten before noon or they do not eat that day.

A special thank you to my little brother of the Big Brother Program David Futrowsky. David has been my little brother since he was 13 years old and he is now 55 years old. He has been a good student for 42 years.

A special thank you to Virginians for Alternatives to the Death Penalty and International CURE

(Citizens United for Rehabilitation of Errants). I have been a long-time member of both groups and their work to stop the execution of prisoners as well as to end the human rights abuses of them and their families and the guards by government officials. My work with them brought me to visit Virginia's death row and to write to some prisoners, such as Joe Giarratano, who likely is innocent of killing two people. Joe would write to me while he was in solitary confinement for some 10 years or so. All is Dharma. All is Practice. All is imperfect perfection.

A special acknowledgement for the Florida Community of Mindfulness Prison Outreach Program and the Southern Palm Zen Group's Prison Program. They are teaching the Dharma at weekly sittings and at special Days of Mindfulness. The Southern Palm Zen Group has a program to train and ordain prison practitioners as lay teachers (at Hardee Correctional Institute, which I tried to visit monthly with other volunteers). FCM sponsors groups at Charlotte CI and Zephyrhills CI. The solid volunteers for these programs are: Chris Gahles, Nancy Cunningham, Alex Lerner, Wilbur Mushin May, and Andrew Solis. For SPZG's program: Rick Ferris, Billy Wetherington, Mary Duncan, Mitchell Doshin Cantor, Wilbur Mushin May, and Jane Jishin Faysash.

Special thanks to the Sunday Farm Sitting and Discussion Group that met monthly at Doug King's grandfather's old cabin in the woods in Land O' Lakes, Florida. We had great Dharma discussions, and would pick oranges to take home when we parted.

Special thanks to the many doctors, nurses, technicians, administrative helpers, ambulance EMTs (these many hidden Bodhisattvas) I have encountered in the new world of cancer as well as ataxia that I have just entered.

My government work mentor and Dharma mentors who introduced me to Thay: Michael Cronin and his wife Ellen. They gave me Thay's book *Peace is Every Step* and told me about Thay's retreat at Front Royal, Virginia. I read the book and went to the retreat, and was changed forever. Interestingly, my bunkmate was a father whose young son had cancer.

At the retreat I had my first mindful meals, sitting, and walking. One meal was macaroni and cheese. Wow, did it taste good. Although I tried to stay hidden in the background because I was not sure I was doing things mindfully correct, I found myself alone one day with Thay in a hallway. I was doing mindful walking down this long corridor and who should be coming up from the other way but Thay! I was going to turn around like I made a mistake and had not intended to walk this way. But I knew Thay would see through this little maneuver to avoid him. So I continued until we met each other. He stopped and smiled and looked into my essence. I said to myself, "Oh my, he sees all of my garbage." If he did, it did not matter. He just smiled a wonderful healing smile while bowing to me, and I to him, and we continued our healing walking.

Later, in April of 2001, I penned this poem:

BOWING

How wonderful,
The honor and privilege
To bow
To your teacher,
Loved-one, friend,
Even a stranger
Or an enemy.
To the Buddha-to-be
Within each one.

With palms together,
As if holding a flower,
That is bending toward them,
As you look into their eyes
To their soul
To become one.

ABOUT THE AUTHOR

William P. Menza

William "Bill" P. Menza (1941 - 2015) was born north of Boston, Massachusetts and lived throughout the United States, most notably in Boston, northern Virginia, New Hampshire, and Florida. He held degrees in sociology and journalism and was a career civil servant in public health and safety. Throughout his life he dedicated his time and energies to reducing the suffering of others and was passionate about giving voice to the suffering of those denied a voice. In his spare time he volunteered with multiple organizations to abolish the death penalty and free prisoners of conscience, wrote poetry, researched genealogy, and devoutly corresponded with family and friends. A devoted student and instructor of Buddhism and meditation, he helped start and supported meditation groups in multiple states, and practiced with meditation groups in Florida, New England, and the Washington, D.C. region. He was ordained into the Order of Interbeing as a Dharmacharya – a Dharma teacher – by Zen Master Thich Nhat Hanh and given the name True Shore of Understanding.

FOR MORE ABOUT THE LIFE AND
TEACHINGS OF THICH NHAT HANH

www.plumvillage.org

28973866R00155

Made in the USA
Middletown, DE
02 February 2016